Sidewalk in the Clouds

AFSHIN YADOLLAHI

Sidewalk in the Clouds

Translated by
Caroline Croskery

Printed by CreateSpace
An Amazon.com Company
CreateSpace, Charleston, SC

Contents

7

Part One

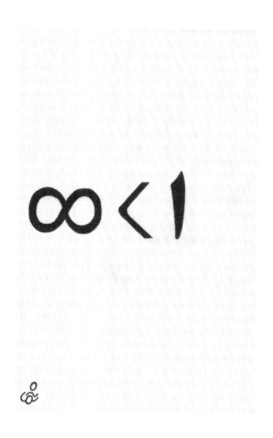

For How Long
Will you
Address me
In the plural "you"
As I am plural
Only with you?

I Write the Word "Rain"
Then the butterflies and wind
Know
Whether it is Autumn or Spring.
~ "Shams Langaroudi"

For Me Writing the Rain Isn't Enough
You must rain
For me to overflow.

Is merely writing
The word rain
Enough for you
Whether in Autumn or Spring?

Sometimes Silence

Isn't words unspoken
It is a wish
Turned into a yearning
By one's own hands.

You
Cannot go on
Loving someone
Who has been gone
For years.

You
Do not belong
To someone
Who is long

Gone.

You
Cannot call
Your lingering
Pain
Love.

You can
Be beholden
For your wounds
But can't still
Need the one who wounded you!
No!
Forget these trifling tales
That in the name of Love
Deprive you
Of Love.

He who
Wants you
As his wounded
Is not your man.
He is not human.

And
For years
You have been
An Adamless Eve
Without realizing it.

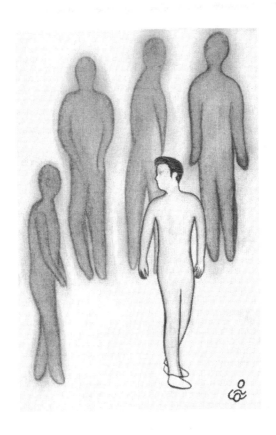

Every Time You Utter
The plural "You"
I look around myself
And see no one there.
I can't figure out
If you are crazy
Or me.

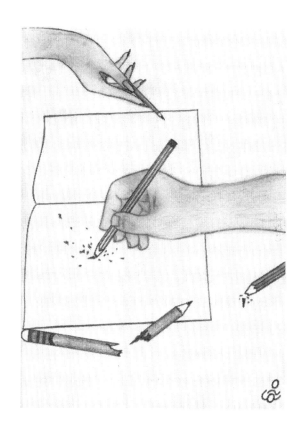

Save My Poetry -

For their peak moments
Are too few.
Save my peak moments -
For their poetry is rare.
And I will save you -
For your peak moments
And poetry
Are rare.

The Alleyways
Won't reach you.
The roads –
Perhaps...

Wandering
Is enough.
I must travel.

Night
Cannot compete with your brightness.
And you
Cannot compete with your own darkness.

Are you brighter than the day
Or darker than the night?

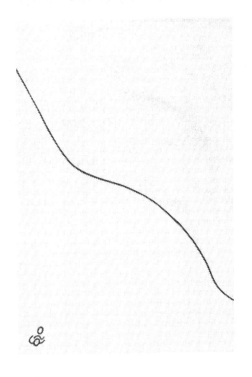

God –
How did He
Sculpt you?
That the curves
Of your body
Are the image
Of my desire?
The waves of your body
Draw me
Into a whirlpool -
Drowning in it
Is inevitable.

Even When You're Sitting
A storm is revealed
In the serenity
Of your figure.

I've gotten lost
In all these calm volcanoes
In the simple stripes on your dress
And you
Are sitting there
Smiling.

Neither before your storm
Is there calm –
Nor afterwards.

O Stormy Calm!

You Have Propped Up the Sun

On your right hand
And brushed the night
Out of its face.
The sun smiles
But the night can be seen
In its eyes...

In the Arms of a Statue

You smile -
The statue also smiles.
Its smile
Is more real
Than yours.

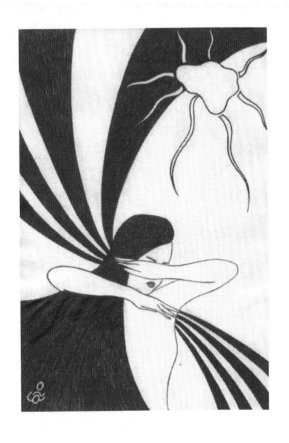

Your Smile
Seems to cry.
You are becoming more charming
And more sad.

You are a black and white
Rainbow
But the silence of your lips
Is red.

When you peek out
The sun
On your face
Slips away –
Not knowing what to do.
It's afraid and...
It goes.

I don't show
Your tranquil face
To anyone –
I'm afraid.
It's hard to let go of you.

Smiling
Is futile.
A person who can read your heart
Needs not look at your face.
Against him
You have nowhere
To run and hide.

Don't be afraid –
He doesn't want to have your secrets

But he only wants to arrange them.
Those that even you have not seen -
He will show you -
He will kiss you -
And anticipate your hands.
And against his security
You are utterly defenseless...

Like You're Looking at a Camera
But
You're looking at nothing at all.

Your eyes
Are nearsighted
And you
Draw near to no one
And you even

Distance yourself
From the mirror.

You just look -
Seeing
Is hard
For you.

Your Body

Is polar –
If you undress at a pole
Date palms will grow among the icebergs
The world will become warm
A thousand leagues away from you

My eyes melt
And your nakedness
Has drowned everything I have

Since you
Far away from me
Have brought the sun
Near the earth.

At Night
You sleep with my lyrics
In the morning
You awaken with your dazed self
Lost in the passageways of your mind
You see me
You do not greet me
And you go on
You have not yet started on yourself

But I
Have started on you.

You Always Used to Avoid Mirrors
And now
You see them
All around yourself
And still don't realize what has changed.
You are just beginning...

On One Side of the Glass

Are you
And on the other side
The fish
You
Step lightly and glide
And the awestruck fish
Watch you swimming
They realize the ocean
Is on the other side of the glass

Where Do You Wander

Until the middle of the night
To escape yourself...
Oh Sun!
Wherever you set foot
It lights up.
Look within yourself.
The mirrors,
The days,
Won't get so bored.

I Don't Hear Your Voice
I see it

Not with my eyes
But with every cell of my being

Not when you're near
But from afar
I see how it inspires my poems
Not only

After composing them
But before!
I see what it does with my longing.
Before I desire,
I see.

Your Voice

Reads my poems
Before they
Are composed.

Your voice
Composes my poems
And I read
The poetry
Of your voice

And all of these
Happen without me
Hearing your voice.

When You Wear Black Like the Kaaba

God, dressed in white
Revolves around you like a Haji

The devil
Happily sheds tears
Under the pebbles they throw at him
And the angels
Feel the time has come to disobey,
When people,

Dumbstruck
In worship of you,
Lose their self-control.
When you wear black
It sets off
A turbulent chaos.

What Are You Going to the Forest For?

You've already set the whole city ablaze!
Isn't that enough?

Your heat
Comes through your doubting gaze...
Trust our love!
Set the whole world ablaze!

What are you going to the forest for?
The city is burned
It can't rise from the ashes like a Phoenix
Unless by your hand.

What are you going to the forest for?
When the trees see you
Cupid, heart shot with arrow
Appears carved upon their trunk

Each tree you sit under
Hugging your knees
Flourishes even more verdant
Warm, warmer
And ignites...

As you sit there hugging your knees
You don't hint of the fire
You are the fire yourself!
You know
One mustn't start fires near trees.

What are you going to the forest for?
You need no firewood
With those devilish eyes!
Let God, after all
Have someplace to hide.

You Wear a Short Skirt

High heels
In your hands
Barefoot
Standing on the desert sands

Under the shade of your tousled hair
You drink and smile

No one
Knows of an oasis
As beautiful
As this one.

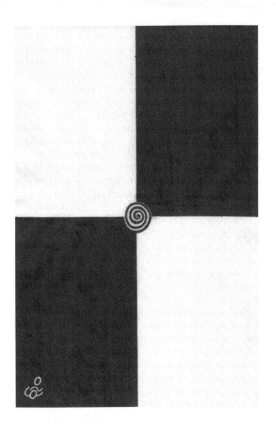

I Feel

God is looking at me through your eyes
And the devil
Is calling to me
From your lips.

And sometimes
These two
Change places.

The right hand
Is God reaching out to me
And the left hand,
The devil.

And sometimes
These two
Change places.

You breathe
The devil in.
You exhale
And release
God.
And sometimes
These two
Change places.

Your heart beats
To their steps -
One beat God,
One beat the devil.

With your Godly body
You light fires.
And with your devilish spirit
You ignite the flames.

At the point when
God and the devil
Come together,
Your thighs begin

And your destiny is determined.
Hell
Is under your feet -
Heaven also...

And sometimes
These two
Change places.

This Dragon is Awakening
And will take from you
Vengeance
For all the years
You deceived it.

Vengeance
For all the unwelcome
Dreams and lullabies

You sang to it
Deceitfully.

Vengeance
For its trust in you
And your nontrust
In it.

You still don't know well
But
The deed is done.

Your fear is
For this reason.
You sense an awakening.
You feel
Its incandescence
In the depths of your soul.
From the very place
Where
You exiled it
From sleep,
By the fire
That was consumed
By the ashes.

I know
Your dragon
Would never have awoken
By yelling.
It needed a whisper
By that hand
That I

Only I
Know
And without your permission
Whispered to it.

Now whatever it is that you want
Ask it of me.
Be perplexed!
Be afraid!

The deed...
Is done.
The fire will enflame.

And your ruin
Of paper
Will rebuild again.
You can now
Draw near
To the mirror.
Look!
You will see the dragon.

And then take me
Into the arms of your flames
So that I
Can turn it into
A rose garden
With a whisper that I, only I know.

Leave it Unanswered

The silence –
It has a thousand meanings.
And I know the correct meaning.
You know it too
And this simplifies
Your dealings with me
And with yourself
Makes them difficult.

Leave it unanswered
Until you see the answer
In my eyes.

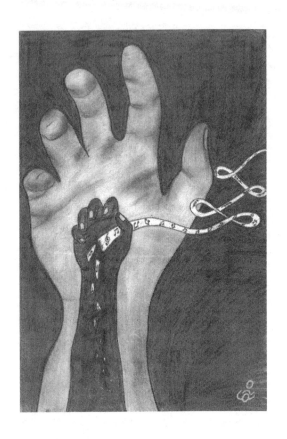

The Waves
Steal your voice
Mid-air.

And I
Still have hope
In an illusion.

You're Not Here

Not here
Not here

Don't you miss me?
Or
Are you running away
From the fear
Of missing me more?

The Clock Stopped
Yesterday morning at 4:23
Time
Ticked
Life
Poetry
All stopped
At 4:23
Yesterday morning.

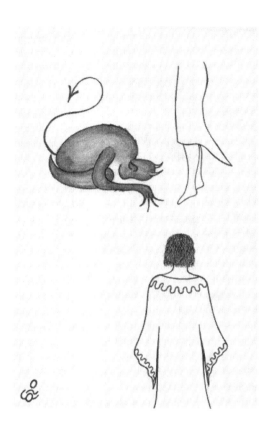

If God
Had created you
Before Adam
The devil
Would have bowed down
To you.

You Took Advantage
Of my trust.
You used
My own words
Against me.
You made me love you
With my poetry.

You Are Not Here Completely
With me tonight.
But I want
All of you.

When you are not
Here completely,
I am not complete.

You are incomplete tonight
And your excuses
Intensify
Your incompleteness.

You have brought me
To the brink of passion.
So understand
That I understand
Nothing
But all of you.

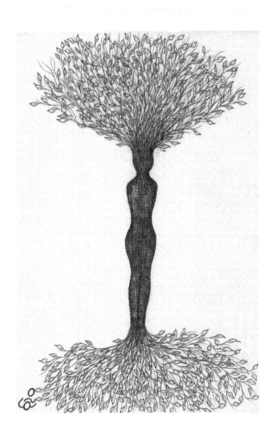

The Irony of You, the Poem

Not reciting poetry!
Poets becoming poets
In your arms,
And you, unaware
Of the land
Of your inspiration.

Your look
Your voice

Your silence
Your tears
Your smile
Being poems,
And you turning away
From the mirror
Lest it show you
Your self
Lest a poem
Be born,
Lest others
See all of you.

What have you seen
In the un-you
That you have grown so accustomed to?
I will discover
All of you
And you
Will sing
Poetry.

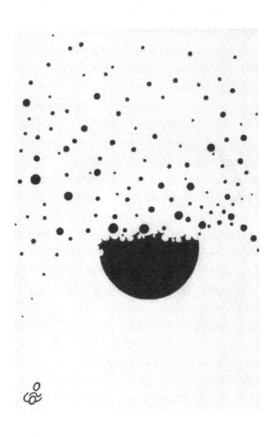

Are You Afraid
I will discover you?
Don't be afraid!
I have discovered you.

The Sidewalk

Rides on the clouds
Every time you
Walk upon it.
It feels like
The Milky Way
That would be simply
A sidewalk
If *you* walked on it.

You Stare Straight Ahead

But the past wells up in your eyes
You are standing
On the threshold of an open cage
But freedom
Means nothing to you.
Clawing at the door frame
And its imaginary safety...
Your lips are red

From your bleeding heart
Your heart still
Is hopeful
That whenever you please
You will go
And your heart is sad
That you want to leave,
But you don't.

Outside
Whatever the season,
It is always Autumn
In the cage
You are yellow
Thinking of falling
Not flying
Leaning your head
Against the threshold
Feeling no hope,
You have fallen in love
With your jailer-
A jailer that is no longer here
And has lost the key to the cage
Many years ago
In you.

A Little Girl

Whose smile
Everyone bought for pennies,
Believing her smile
Not worth more,
She thought she would be worthless
Without it.

She didn't talk, she smiled.

She didn't complain, she smiled.
She didn't cry, she smiled.

And one day
When they bought all of her smiles
Below cost,
They scoffed at her and left
When she had no smiles left.

The Ocean
Is beside you.
It reaches out its hand
As a pier
Toward you.

You sit facing yourself
With your back to it
Not answering it
As it holds its breath

Drowning in you.

A little later
In this deadening silence
Only
A few of its teardrops
Are left... on the pier.

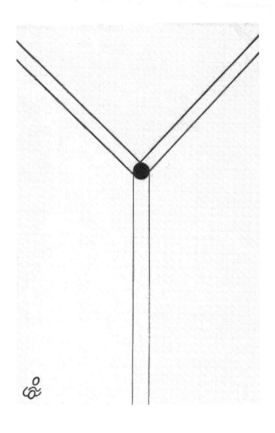

As You Look Up to the Sky

the Mystics,
who have kissed the whole world goodbye,
are given
their most difficult test:
a neck
that neither can they kiss -
nor put aside.
But I know
how I would answer

74

that test.
I would kiss it
And never put it aside.

Something
That God Himself
Wishes for.

You Have a Problem

Living under a roof,
And so do the birds.

Come up to the rooftop
To fly
Whenever you wish.

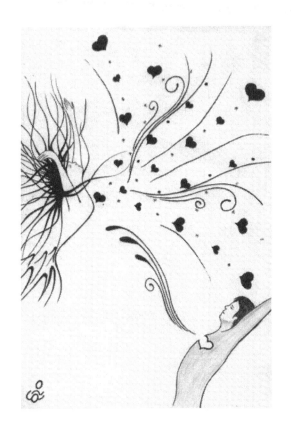

You Have Shaped an Empty Heart

With your fingers.
You hold it over your head
And show it to me.
You say, "It's yours."

Are you showing me
My heart's empty space?
Are you reminding me

My heart isn't in its place?
Are you teasing me?
You are right.
You have won.
But I am still alive
Without a heart.

I realize now
How much better life is
Without a heart.

And you must
Carry the heavy burden
Of my heart
On your shoulders.

I am right.
I am the winner.

Yet you tease me?

The Pigeons in Your Courtyard

Awaken you
When pecking at their seed
In the early morning.
You scatter food
For them
And think of them.

And for many years

Mornings and nights
Your heart pecks
Inside your chest
But you don't awaken
Or even shed one tear for it
Nor think of it.

Kind yet unkind!

You Are a Wellspring in a Wasteland

And I am very thirsty
When I reach you.

I drink from all of your springs.

You are a wellspring
And you can quench my thirst
But you only fan its flames
To make your spring
More bubbly.

Don't Fill Up Our Moments
With an Ellipsis -
Three dots on a line.
Don't leave any
Empty spaces.

These empty spaces
Will fill up with sorrow -
With others.

Ellipsis is not silence,
It is longing
It is anger
It is absence.

Talk to me
Fill this space.
Never let your place
be empty.

From the Beginning of the Night
I have seen tears
In your voice.

I told you so
But you
Denied it.
I see you
Without

Seeing you.

Your scent was
Of crying.

And Your heart
Told me
"She is not well"
Before you spoke.

It was talking about you
And it wanted me
To make you cry
To lighten your burden.

Forgive me
If your heart
And I conspired together.
It was for your own sake.

Cry tonight.
Everything is ready
Except my presence
To embrace you
While you cry.

But there is nothing we can do.
Your tears are much too heavy
To wait
Until that day.

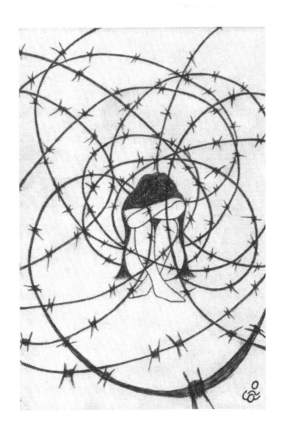

You Are Afraid
Of a caress.

You have the right to be.

Touching
Will make your old wounds
Scream,
Old wounds

That perforate your world
Like an ellipsis.

Don't be afraid
I won't caress you
But will make you
Touch yourself
Little by little
And then
You will caress me
And we
Will caress each other.

Tonight
Don't Lose Sleep
For anyone

Sleep
For me!

I Sleep and Entrust My Night to You

My dreams
To your awakening
To your dreams
For you to do with them
Whatever you desire.
Until morning
My world
Is yours.

Wherever You Are
The Prime Meridian is there
And time is zero
At that very place.

The world sets
It's time to you
And the Prime Meridian
Runs right between
My eyes.

It Was Night

And night
And again, night -
Like there was no end to it.

It was humid
And cool,
Fragrant
And deep.

There was no image
But
All of the other senses
Took hold
Very gently

I felt the night
On my face
Like the black chiffon
Of love
That took on the scent of heaven
From the dew
Of a trembling body
Drowning me
Moment by moment.

Suspension in the safety of freedom,
In the weightlessness
Of time standing still,
While I lay beside her -
And her hair
Covered the whole world.

Sleep with Me
I live
With you
In my sleep.

Go Prancing About

Steal hearts
Peek out
Hide
Sleep
Tease
Kill
Bring back to life
Build
Destroy...

I will serenade you.
I don't mind
Any of the things you do
I adore them
When serenading you.

So carry on
And let me sing.

In Our Memories
The space for travel
Is empty.

The space for a whole day
Beside each other
Is empty.

The space for wandering the streets

To our heart's desire
Is empty.

Spending a few moments
In carefree conversation
Is empty.

The space of a kiss
Is empty.

And we're still
In love
We still have
Imageless memories
Voiceless memories
They become poems
Become drawings
Travel
Wandering
Talking
Kissing

And others all
Share
Our memories.

Women Like You

Make up for
The ugliness
Of the universe.

I mean that
A woman like you
Makes up for
The ugliness
Of the universe.

I'm just trying to say
That *you*
Make up for
The ugliness
Of the universe.

You are the mercy of fate
By which
God redeems Himself.

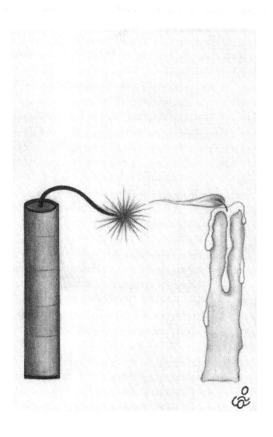

Will You Give
Your lips
To me?

Don't ask what for
When you already know.

I know
That trusting
Is hard for you.

But
If
I were never to kiss you
How much would you trust me?
A man that seeing you
And dreaming of kissing you
Wouldn't make him
Lose control?

How could you trust
A man who would never kiss you
Without your permission
So that
You could know
The pleasure
Of making a man crazy
And as you push him away
With your
Enticing gaze,
In your smiling heart
You are eager
For the next time
He loses control.

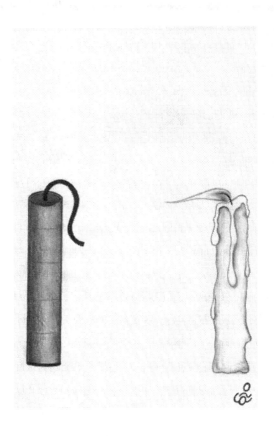

Don't Be Afraid
Of me
Find a corner
Far from me
And keep busy.

In my mind
I have kissed you
A thousand times
A thousand times...

And
And I have repeated
This a thousand times
A thousand times over
Without ever telling you
Without ever
Asking anything
Of you.

Without you meaning to,
And with you not meaning to,
You spread madness.

So sit over there
Away from me
And stay busy
With your own business.

I have everything
To do with you
Yet nothing to do with you.

You are safe
Within my safety
And I am safe
Within your danger.

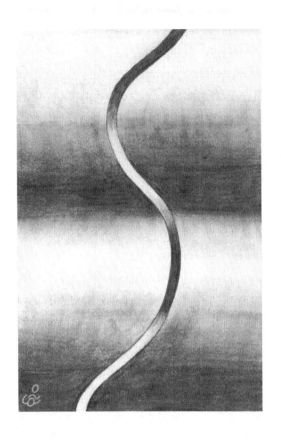

If You Were Here
I would die
in your arms
until dawn
and then
come alive
in them
again
in the morning.

When You Put Your Hands on Your
Head
The world heads into your hands.

Don't take your hands off your head!
Don't unhand the world!
Let it spin!

Gravity is the handiwork
Of this headiness
Otherwise not a pebble
Would stay in place.

And love
Is your hands
That do not
Unhand the world.

With Your Empty Place Beside Me

Closing my eyes
Is not called sleep.
It's a temporary death
That makes me forget your absence
For a few hours.

And if it weren't for your memory
The nightmares

Would make me wish for wakefulness;

The same thing
Your empty place beside me
Does to me
When I am awake.

When You Leave Without Saying a
Word
The mirror mis-fastens
The buttons of its shirt.

My shoes go out

When I leave the house,
I forget to take myself along.

My string of momentary prayer beads
Breaks
And the beads fall like tears
All over the ground.

When you come home
You fasten my buttons straight.

My shoes arrive home
Right before
You do.

Bead by bead
You pick my moments
Up off the ground.
You restring them...

And when I'm beside you,
I need no mirror
Or shoes
Or shirt
Or tears
Or moments...

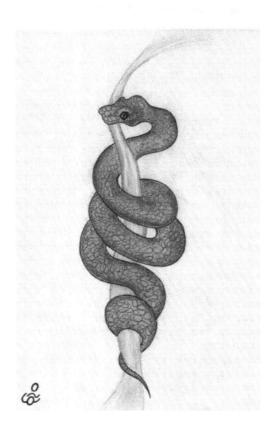

My Heart Misses an Embrace
That is a Misses' embrace.

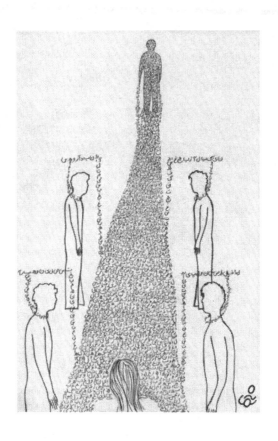

I Said Send Me a Poem -
But not the poems
That others recite to you;

Not the poems
Where they lay down their lives
Because of you.

I said to send me a poem
But now I say,

118

Send me the poem
Of whoever writes you eloquently,
Even if from another beau.

I want to know
How lofty those who love you write
How deeply they love
How far they have traveled
Down the road
On which
I stand waiting
At the end.

I Sleep
Next to your empty place every night,
Next to your absence,
Next to not having you.

And you sleep in your own emptiness
every night,
In your own absence
In not having yourself.

And he sleeps
Next to you every night,
Next to your absence,
Next to not having you.

Each one of us
In some way
Doesn't have you,
Who is more alone
Than any of us.

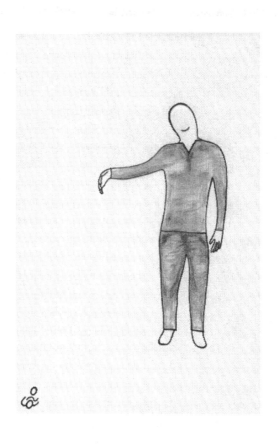

My Heart is Happy
despite your empty place –
because it is *your* empty place.

She Said Probably

I'll be home sooner than usual,
But she was not
Home sooner.

Not that she didn't want to.
It wasn't in her hands.
She had to wait.
And she waited for many years,
So long

That it seemed
She never returned.

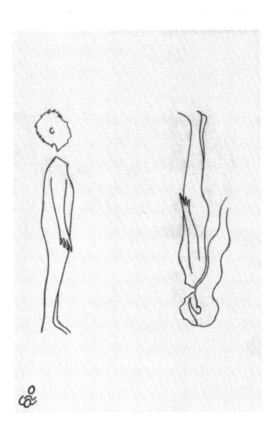

You Are Dying From Sleep
And I am dying,
From wakefulness.

Our similarity
Is that
We are both dying,
In sleep
And wakefulness.

Your Lips

Know my kiss
Like Eve's lips
Knew Adam's.
But for Eve
There was no other Adam.
But for you
There are
Many other Adams,
But none of those Adams

Are like me
For you.

So you are even more Eve
Than Eve
and I, more Adam
Than Adam,
Which means
That we will never
Return
To the Garden of Eden.

Tonight
What unfinished business
Did you go after
That you returned
More unfinished?

For what guilty feeling
Were you trying
To atone,
That you came home

Even more guilty?

What conviction
Made you
More indecisive?

Your chaotic silence
is
everywhere.

How do you interpret
The mingling
Of your wonder and smile?

What do you expect
Of me?

I don't grin
but bear it in silence.
I wait.

On the day that I see you
Your eyes will tell me
Everything they have seen.

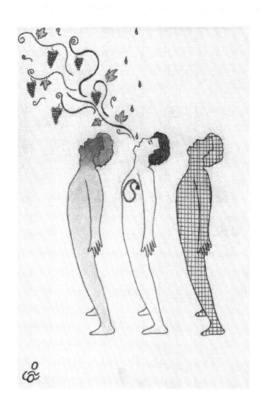

She Cried Tears
I drank them.

My mouth
Had the scent of wine,
My body
Of deliverance,
My past
Took on the color of oblivion,
My future
The color of disgrace.

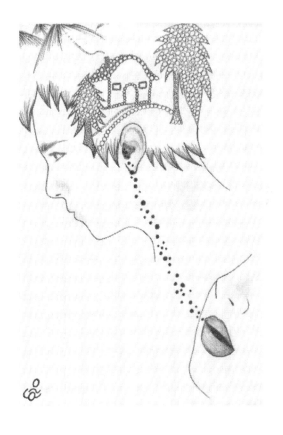

I Believe Your Lies

Come!
Let's arrange
For the truth
To be these very lies
That you tell me.

With Your Hair

You veil your face,
Your figure
Like a gown
That adorns
All of you.

When you wear your hair
Like winter's longest night
The mystery of your nudity

Pulls my restraint
To disgrace.

Your wear your hair
Like a gown.
Don't take it off!
Let the black chiffon
Soften
The usual distance
Between us.

It Seems In a Moment

That I conquer
The Seven Wonders of the World
And their history -
And I feel
Every heartbeat
In every land -
And I taste
All of the love
From the beginning of time

Until the end of days
When I kiss you.

Have You Hidden the Cloudy Skies
Behind the rain?
How can there be rain
Without clouds?
Rain!
Let the clouds
Disappear
Drop by drop.

The moon is waiting.

The Persian New Year's Table
Of the "seven S's"
Is nothing
Next to your Soul
Next to your Simplicity
Next to your Scarlet lips
Next to your Sable eyes
Next to your Silence
Next to your years of Solitude

And Stoic Smile
Mirrored by each other
Next to your book of life
Next to your name...

Be my seven S's
And I will write
The rest of your book of life
Beside your warm smile,
In quiet moments together,
Where every day
Is New Year's Day.

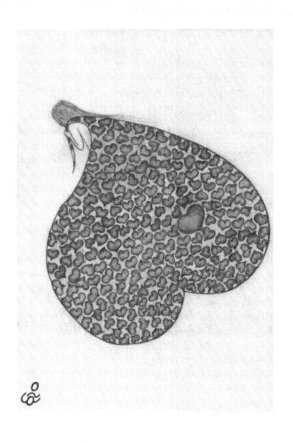

You Don't Realize It
Doesn't
the burden of so many poets -
Of so many poems
Weigh heavy on your shoulders?

But I am thinking of you.
I love you
And I won't write poems for you anymore.

The lighter your load,
The easier the end will be.

You yourself don't realize it.

Is It Possible to See You

And not write poems
For you?
What poet
Would deny himself
That chance?

All of the poets
Seeing you
Would burst forth in poetry for you

For their plight
Even unintentionally
But
You
Must
Only
Read my poems.
Let the others be.

Let just once
The lover command the beloved:
You must read
Only my poems.

You Whose Heat
Can make
Date palms grow
On icebergs,
Can be so cold as to
Make icicles form
On date palms
At the equator.

Your Beauty
Is so intense
That
You have the right
To break any law.

Break them!
You are always
In the right...

When You Are Sad
Bodies prepare
To confess.

When you smile
God
Gives humanity a second chance.

Judgment Day
Is postponed.

You Have the Right

To expect them
To stare at you
From thousands of windows.

However great
However bright
I am no more than
One window.

When You Say
I am incomparable
It makes me sad.

I realize
That you have compared me.

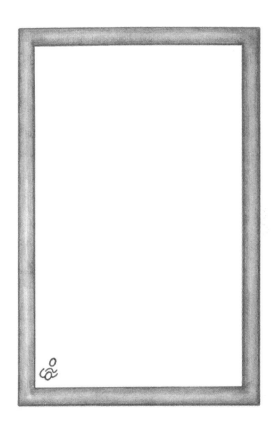

Your Beauty
Without exaggeration
Is as great as
The women in paintings
Whose beauty
Has been exaggerated.

Part Two

I Am Just Now Getting to Know
Who you are
Because
I don't know
Who you are
Anymore.

For Hours
I wait
For you to come.

When you arrive
I realize
The hours don't wait
For hours.

Time
Has been lost
You
Have been lost
I
Have been lost

When the hours
Don't wait
For hours

It Was Too Soon
for her to go.
It became too late
To return.

It started
With difficulty
But ended
Easily.

Started
With purpose -
Ended
For no reason.

Everything bad
Seemed good
And everything good
Seemed bad.

But I'm fine now
Because
In this short time
I did not fall short.
I hope
She will be well.
I hope
Her next time
With the next person
Won't be so short.

As for me,
I'm used to shortness.

That Lump Doesn't End in Your
Throat

When it takes hold of your eyes
Tears come
But don't fall.

When it takes hold of your chest
Your breath
Neither comes
Nor goes.

When it takes hold of your heart
It huddles in a corner
Doesn't beat
But quivers.

The hand either
Becomes a fist
Or is revealed.

The feet
Are in limbo
Between staying and going.

When the lump breaks
These things
Just change places
But nothing really changes.

That lump
Is the only thing

That doesn't break
when it breaks.

Little by Little
I'll have to doubt
Those decent people
Around you
These days.

It's not their fault
But
This
Is one of the bad traits
That you have.

You are contagious
Those poor fellows
Get lovesick
And then
There's no telling
What they're capable of.

I know
Since I got it from you.

When You Are Inattentive to Me,
Your mind is elsewhere.

A person is where the mind is.

When She's Busy

She gets tipsy,

When she gets tipsy
She is even more busy.

With the people she gets busy with
She gets more tipsy,

With the people she gets tipsy with
She gets even more busy.

She forgets
That she has someone who loves her;
Someone she used to love.

When you ask about her
She answers like a person
Whose heart has grown cold.
She doesn't say much
But what she doesn't say
Says much.

Your love grows idle
By her busyness.

You don't want to ruin
Her busyness.
You leave her busy
With her happiness.

And you should
No longer

Put much hope
In someone loving you.

Save yourself!

No News
Time after time...

She is everywhere
Except with you.

They all console her
Take care of her
And she feels so bad
That
She cannot
Talk to you
She can't even
Answer
Your call
Or
Your message.

No news
Time after time.

She feels so bad
That they suddenly
Take her on a trip
And you
Find out about it

When she's almost there.

No News
Time after time.

She only planned to be gone
For a day
And that one day
Was so long
As if your plans with her
Were never planned.

No News
Time after time.

She returns
And she still feels bad.
She's still not alone.
And the neighbor she never
Even had until yesterday
Is now always there
More than her father
More than you
And you
Still don't know what happened.

No News
Time after time.

Suddenly
She buys a car.
Suddenly
She has a get-together.

Suddenly
She cuts her hand.
Suddenly
She's putting you on hold.
Suddenly
She's making excuses.
Suddenly
She's never online.
Suddenly
She comes online
But
Not for you.

In the real world
New things are happening
Suddenly.

No News
Time after time.

And you
Dare not write her poetry
Because
Suddenly
She's breathless
And down
And this
Is your fault
With your wordplay
That you know well
How to do.

It would be better

If you knew well
What to do with silence
What to do
With "suddenly"
What to do
With
No news
Time after time.

I Was Always There For Her

She was never there for me.

At the beginning
I used to call this
Love
And now
I call it love.

"Love" has no meaning.

I Know

You always think about me.
I feel
That you are overwhelmed
By memories
Of me
Because
Neither in the morning
Do you find the time to say "Good
Morning"

Nor at night
The time to say "Goodnight."

I say nothing
Lest
You lose
Your focus
On me.

I have
Never been
So
Comfortable
With anyone.

A Burn
Is a burn
Whether on the lips
Or on the hand
Or on the heart.

If a scar is left behind
It doesn't matter where -
You remember.

How Would You Feel
If you found out
You were someone's worst friend?
Would you smile

162

Or
Shrug it off?

I Don't Make Wishes at Night

For you to sleep well
Anymore
When you are awake all night.

From tonight
I will wish
That you enjoy your night life
So that
My wishes
Won't stand
In the way
Of yours.

When Everything is Half Done

The halves
Don't add up -
They subtract
From each other.

When Poetry Becomes Wordplay

And the poet,
Becomes the person who
Knows how to use poetry,
Suddenly

The words
Topple over your head
And
Your breath is cut off
Under the weight of emotions
You are left holding
In your hands.

When they don't
Say "God Keep You"
They mean
"Goodbye"

Meaning
You and God know....

She is right.

See the story of poets' love
When the time comes
Not at any time
Did any poem
Save any love.

Wordplay
Is not poetry!

These Days
You've grown accustomed
To being cold
And saying
"It's nothing"

To me asking
And you saying
"It's nothing"

You leaving suddenly
And I seeing
That it's nothing.

You're right.
It's nothing.

I was wrong to think
It was something.

It's nothing.

In Love
It's not good news
When there is
No news.

In Love
No news
Is not good news.

In Love
News
Means
Someone still
Thinks of you

Even
If
She doesn't know it
And
No news
Means
She will never
Think of you
Again
Even if
She doesn't know it.

"No news"
Is not good news.

Your Tears Smiled
Without you knowing.

I tasted them
With my eyes.

They were sweet

Unlike your smile
That cried
Without you
Knowing it.

I tasted them
With my ears.

They were bitter.

What a waste
That I was fasting
From love,
Otherwise
I would have drunk them
So they wouldn't
Stain your skirt;
The sweet wine
That washes over
Your affected smile,
Becomes bittersweet
And dark.

I Know a Sensitive Woman

Who killed
Yesterday's lover
With a poisonous love
And she cries in the arms
Of today's lover
Remembering
The love she killed
While
She schemes the murder
Of her present lover
For whom she will
Cry in memory
In the arms of tomorrow's lover.

A woman who
Will never reach satisfaction.

Now I Understand
Why
Any man who falls in love
With you
Or you
Fall in love with him,
Undergoes metamorphosis
Is banded,
And dies.
This is not a strange thing
For Arachnids that have bands on their
legs-
You are just like female spiders.

But at the threshold of death
I was able to escape metamorphosis
And not become banded.
Poor male spiders!

About the Author

Afshin Yadollahi is a distinguished Iranian poet, songwriter and composer born in 1969 who completed his graduate studies with a Ph.D. in Psychiatry and currently works in this field of medicine.

Afshin Yadollahi's prolific works have contributed to numerous radio and television programs and Iranian feature films, which have made him one of Iran's most successful song writers. His works are lasting contributions to every genre including pop, classical and traditional Iranian music.

His works also have been translated and published in Russian and French.

Other Collections by Afshin Yadollahi:

Logical Passion
Sleep With My Poems Tonight
Things I Had to Say and You Had to Hear
Patron of a Closed Tavern

172

About the Translator

Caroline Croskery was born in the United States and moved to Iran at the age of twenty-one. She holds a Bachelor's Degree from the University of California at Los Angeles in Iranian Studies where she graduated with distinction. For many years, she has been active in three fields of specialization: Language Teaching, Translation and Interpretation and Voiceover Acting.

During her thirteen years living in Iran, she taught English and also translated and dubbed Iranian feature films into English. After returning to live in the United States, she began a ten-year career as a court interpreter and translator of books from Persian into English. She is an accomplished voiceover talent, and currently continues her voiceover career in both English and Persian.

Caroline Croskery has translated and narrated a variety of other titles.

Novels:

We Are All Sunflowers, by Erfan Nazarahari

Democracy or Democrazy, by Seyed Mehdi Shojaee

In the Twinkling of an Eye, a collection of short stories by Seyed Mehdi Shojaee

You're No Stranger Here, by Houshang Moradi Kermani

A Vital Killing: A Collection of Short Stories from the Iran-Iraq War, by Ahmad Dehghan

Stillness in a Storm, by Saeid Ramezani

The Water Urn, by Houshang Moradi Kermani

A Sweet Jam, a novel for children and young adults by Houshang Moradi Kermani

Year of the Tree, a novel by Zoha Kazemi

Made in the USA
Columbia, SC
16 August 2017